CRE]

MW01195520

(FROM PRADA TO NADA)

Volume One

<u>A GUIDE TO RESTORING YOUR SOUL & CREDIT AT THE SAME TIME.</u>

information is without contract or any type of guarantee assurance.

The trademarks that are used are without any consent, and the publication of the trademark is without permission or backing by the trademark owner. All trademarks and brands within this book are for clarifying purposes only and are the owned by the owners themselves, not affiliated with this document.

TABLE OF CONTENTS

INCLUDED GOODIES:

- **SEVEN SIMPLE STEPS**
- **PERSONAL LEARNING WORKBOOK**
- **PROMISED RESOURCES**

Dedication

This book is dedicated to my Lil' brother – "The Bear", you are my inspiration, motivation, and rock! Your harsh words gave me the PUSH to move above and beyond suicide- and Make It Happen! When I didn't think, I could take another breathe because of circumstances you MADE me see differently. You've stood strong and have taken care of many who have left you by the wayside but you always forgave and kept pushing. Most of all you've been my ride or die in TRUE form, staying positive and putting God first in all things. Always remember we have that unstoppable BOND, unmovable FAITH, and Shatterproof LOYALITY that most siblings dream of having. Even when you changed your habits, your ways and your lifestyle that was not good enough for God – so he stepped in, pulled you back only to put his final touches of anointing on you. What we've endured these last 3 seasons were God's "NECESSARY DOSE OF LIFE" so as we move forward and shake off all unneeded and unwanted NEGATIVE ENERGY we move into our Destiny of Focus. We move on to the next level and like *"Creme in coffee"* WE ALWAYS RISE TO THE TOP"!

Glory to **God** we finally got the lesson.

LOVE ALWAYS YOUR BIG *SIS'*

FAVORITE QUOTES:

The unwilling, led by the unknowing, are doing the impossible, for the ungrateful, we have done so much for so long with so little we are now qualified to do anything with nothing.
- **Konstantin Jireček**

"I've never fooled anyone. I've let people fool themselves. They didn't bother to find out who and what I was. Instead they would invent a character for me. I wouldn't argue with them. They were obviously loving somebody I wasn't."
— **Marilyn Monroe**

"And once the storm is over, you won't remember how you made it through, how you managed to survive. You won't even be sure, whether the storm is really over. But one thing is certain. When you come out of the storm, you won't be the same person who walked in. That's what this storm's all about."
— **Haruki Murakami**

Stop watering things that were never meant to grow in your life. Water what works, what's good, what's right. Stop playing around with those dead bones and stuff you can't fix, it's over...leave it alone! You're coming into a season of greatness. If you water what's alive and divine, you will see harvest like you've never seen before. Stop wasting water on dead issues, dead relationships, dead people, a dead past. No matter how much you water concrete, you can't grow a garden.
T. D. Jakes

Surround yourself with people whose definition of you is not based on your history, but your destiny.
T. D. Jakes

No matter what you've been through, no matter what others might have thought about you...you are who God says you are. You are talented, you are a success, and you are an overcomer!
Joel Osteen

Forgive your enemies, but never forget their names.
John F. Kennedy

Acknowledgements

I would first like to thank **God** for the strength & courage he's given me through this whole process and bringing me through to the starting line; I'm humble, grateful and most of all, I'm at peace.

Next, I would like to thank my **Neighbor** who would not fix my credit for me, and forced me to go out and seek resources which lead to an incredible commercial credit brokering business and a book! Which leads me to this awesome person I'd love to thank – **Mike Citron**, from Dispute Suite who told me to write a book and then showed me how. I will never forget **Jenifer Cullen,** who I met at the *"Credit Boot Camp"* and she trusted me enough to put me on her panel to speak. She said, "You said you want to be a motivational speaker, here's your opportunity- Speak!" I would like to acknowledge my **Mom** who always continues to support me through her voice of wisdom. To my Dad whose spirit is continuously surrounding my space. To my **Twins** who forced me off the sofa and made me look at myself – they told me I was a *winner* & supported my efforts. They continue to lift and challenge my motivation and desire to be successful, so I will finish the race! To my **Son** who I was up praying for day & night gave me the extra endurance I needed for this project.

To **Jah**' my confidante and my spiritual advisor, thanks for always making me see the glass 1/2 full. To my nephew **Suggie**, who always tried to find words to comfort me in my times of distress, your unwavering love is so appreciated. To my **Aunt Cookie**, without you I just don't know what I would have done. To my **Aunt Kaye**, who I can call whenever, and ask whatever, you never turned me away. Thanks to my **Uncle Del**, who had my back when I least expected it. To my niece, **Victoria** who helped me put my business in order and is the *epitome* of what dedication means, I love you girl! Finally, to my little **Angels** with wings who gave me a special financial jump start, and believed in me from day one I'll forever be grateful for your generosity.

Introduction

Hello and thank you for buying my book,' 'CREDIT CHRONICLES", (A Life Resource to Restoring your CREDIT & your Soul at the same time.)

This book was written for *real people* who want to better themselves, take control and realize that everyone, and I do mean *everyone,* has a story a past or experiences they have overcome. The truth is our stories serve as lessons for us and as a resource for others to help lead them on the right path. Regardless of this, most of us are not willing or wanting to share, because of the embarrassment, self-incrimination, or stigmatization that accompany telling our stories. Well, I've been one of those people, so embarrassed and humiliated I was afraid to even look at strangers, in the back of my mind I was thinking about if they were going to look me up on google (as if I was so important!)

Not anymore! I'm here to share one of many stories, and give you information that none of the credit repair companies or credit reporting bureaus will mention when it comes to taking care of your **CREDIT HEALTH**. The reason why they only share limited information is because it's a business, and it's all about money. Not only do I want you to be informed about the best way to improve and repair your credit and elevate your credit score, but I want this to be a **SOUL RESTORATION** experience while giving you the knowledge that will enable you go to the next level and then the very next, till you reach a state of stability.

This book is written for those who have been in credit bondage because of bad decisions, lack of discernment, prison, losing everything, death of a loved one and the list goes on. We've all been dealt what I call the necessary dose of life. The difference is what we do next- how we act, what steps we take, and how strong we become after that necessary dose of life.

Please understand that everyone goes through what I call life obstacles, setups or setbacks and disappointments. Even though in the public perception, I should be ashamed and embarrassed about what life has dealt me, I'm not. You see, what I went through was what I consider to be a blessing, going through it was what enabled me to write this book. I see this as the opportunity of a lifetime- the opportunity to help myself and help other people instead of letting **FEAR** paralyze me.

Hopefully, my story will help others get a new lease on life and their credit. You're probably asking how my story can help you get on track. In the seven chapters of this book I will share with you the true story of how not paying attention to my credit health nearly destroyed me. I will show you examples of what I should have done differently, and how "Necessary Life Obstacles" define our lives.

My name is Capri - I have a very captivating but true story I'd like to share now that I'm able to finally hold my head high and let go of fear. I believe the universe is giving me everything I want and need to be able to pass this on to just about everyone who is willing and ready to take hold of it. The words within the following pages are not only true but will keep you on the edge of your seat. To get a little glimpse into my story, in April 2013, I had six figures in my bank account, my twins were in their sophomore year of college and my son was living with his dad. Life was good! I had been an entrepreneur for the last 15 years and I was good at it too- I've owned a real estate investment company, tax business, 2 convenience stores, a restaurant and a bar in the heart of Buckhead... and then things started to go wrong.

In the next chapters I will give you excerpts from my life and how I went from making six figures to spending 15 hours in jail, (believe me when I say those 15 hours felt like 15 long years) and transforming from a fulfilled life to a life of unemployment.

From word to word, paragraph to paragraph, page to page and chapter to chapter, I will give you the insight on how you can be set free from issues related to credit. I will show you how having good credit could have saved me from going to jail, being misled, and fighting for my reputation and most of all my freedom. But like I said before, "Life Obstacles" are very necessary to improve one's future.

I hope you not only enjoy reading this book, but also restore your Soul and Credit at the same time.

NEVER LET YOUR PAST DICTATE YOUR FUTURE!

Chapter 1
Let the "Necessary Life Obstacles" Lessons Begin!

September 2013, Atlanta

Dear God, thank you for always providing for me so that I can take care of my family the best way that I can. As always God I try to remember to put you first in every decision although sometimes I do fall short- please forgive me. Amen

Business was booming, I was happy, my kids were happy (or they seemed happy), life was going well. On one of those days after chit-chatting with my girls, they made it known to me that mother-daughters bonding time was long overdue. I was a single parent and we were very close, but it was unusual for them to be open about such a thing to me, so we decided to fix it. Our plan was to try to spend more time together; have fun like we did before they went away to college. I had also promised to continue to be at every event, cheering them from the front row.

While attending their sorority event that week, I got a call from the accountant that I hired to audit my tax business. He told me there was something wrong with a certain tax preparer's documents and that it was super important that I send every one of her client letters to refer them to the IRS for their refunds. He also instructed me to contact the third-party bank and request that they no longer send this preparer's refunds to our bank. Unfortunately they were not able to return funds back to the IRS.

So, I had to get over $88,000 in cashier's checks to send back to the IRS for the refund money that had been deposited into our account from the IRS for this tax preparer's clients along with a letter stating that our company suspected inappropriate mishandling of those specific returns. I made sure that I included the auditor's findings as well.

At that point I decided to retain an attorney in the state that this preparer lived as a precaution. I needed to protect myself and my business. It eventually turned out that not only was my intuition right, but I should have listened to my own inner-voice in the very beginning. The preparer was involved in so much illegal activity it was mind blowing. One would have thought that since I had done my part to ensure compliance by having all preparers get what they call a PTIN number, so that they would be responsible for anything unethical and it would be their own responsibility to handle, right? I would be okay and my business was safe.

Now let's recap:

1. I ensured all tax preparers had an active PTIN number with the IRS (which is a preparer's tax identification number.)
2. I requested that an audit be performed by a third-party accounting firm
3. I notified all respective parties involved, client, bank, and tax preparer
3. I Contacted the IRS and I returned $88,000
4. I retained an attorney

I had done everything, right? I would be free of someone else's transgressions. Wrong.

It did not matter that I tried to do everything to protect myself, my reputation and my business- the government, system or whatever body that was in charge did not give a hoot! Not only was my business scarred and my reputation painted in beautiful black, but I had also experienced loss from many angles. No, this was just the beginning.

November 2013,

So, it was a no brainer to take advantage of this new business venture, since my daughter was planning to go to med-school at UCLA moving to LA would establish residency to help with the cost. I purchased three traffic schools, which cost me a fortune. It was a big risk, but they were projected to yield me about 3.1 million dollars annually. I can recognize a great opportunity when I come across one. So, I had sold my businesses and house and packed up and moved to LA. My daughter was the main reason for the move but a secondary reason was that things were no longer booming and blooming for me in Atlanta. Most of all I wanted to change my sphere of influence and soar to another height.

I did tell you I was doing well financially when I was in Atlanta, right? Well I was. There are a few things in life that never leave us no matter what the circumstances are.

For me, that thing happened to be my *MILLIONAIRE MENTALITY* and lifestyle. So even though I sold my businesses and did not have a steady flow of income except from my rental properties, my millionaire mindset stayed the same. I believed my drive and determination would always prevail and there's enough money out here for those who want it. My son decided to come back to live with me and we moved into a 5-bedroom house with 4-bathrooms, an Olympic-size swimming pool, and an indoor full-size basketball court. With three cars- my 550 SEL Mercedes, a Range rover and a Mercedes SUV, I was determined to keep living how I was accustomed to living. (Rather than being worried about how God wanted me to live) Looking back now, the girls were gone so why did we need all that stuff?

I spent about $20,000 in moving expenses and 15 thousand in getting licensing and lawyers' fees for my new business

Once we settled in I called Mr. Stewart who was brokering the deal and in charge to finalize the last details of the purchase of the business, but he was nowhere to be found. I could feel my confidence level slowly depleting and my anger meter on 1000! I turned into a CSI Agent after what had seemed like a thousand and one phone calls I finally tracked him down, and the news he gave me was that the owner had sold the same business to someone else. How the hell did that happen? I had a contract, hired an attorney and gave earnest money- I seemed to have done everything right – **WRONG!** He said there was a "loop hole" in my contract. I was now on a relentless search and destroy mission, I even went to this man's (owner) house and left notes for him but he had gone into hiding or something and was nowhere to be found. Where was the integrity not to mention my **damn** earnest money! As I sat out by my poolside in a daze-My heart sank. This was where the *"**Necessary Life Obstacles**"* had started to turn horribly bad. I was determined not to let my children or anyone know what was happening, but this was one time I felt like a Mack truck was just following me around and was trying to push me off a cliff.

That's when my survival skills kicked in, and I managed to dust myself off. I started from scratch and went back to what I knew how to do best, and that was Real Estate.

August 2014,

Now, it seemed my money was quickly evaporating. About the time, I received my real estate license, my mother became emotionally distraught. This was compounded with some other issues she was dealing with and she asked that I come home. My mother loss my father and step-father within a 14-month period and she was very close to both. Coping was hard for her and she was starting to grieve. My mother is very special to me so I didn't hesitate. I packed up my house in pods, put them in storage and made my way to Colorado.

I knew in my heart I would not be going back to L.A. once I finished seeing about my mom.

Those 4 months were the worst time in my life (or so I thought at the time). My mother was so mean to me, it was either she was mad because she thought I was failing in my success or because I could no longer give her an allowance or maybe it had just dawned on her that her husband was really dead- I don't know. I got a part-time job at Sak's because my mother drove me insane and I couldn't focus on anything. Getting a job was an opportunity for me to stay out of her way, besides my girls were in college and I paid their rent and all their expenses which included out-of-state tuition, so I had to do something to make a little money. I had started to experience loss from many angles. This was still only the beginning.

Chapter 2
Time to Pick Up the Pieces!

December 2014, Atlanta

Dear God, I need to know you are listening and hearing my prayers. Time is getting a little rough and I need your guidance to show me the way, and I mean the right way. Amen

I was back in Atlanta trying to gain my momentum back. My funds were basically gone, and it was hustle time! I landed a job working for a bank selling B2B banking products. After working for myself for so long it felt weird working as an employee, but I had to work to take care of the twins who were in college and my son was also trying to make something of himself. I needed to be in Atlanta where my connections were, so I stayed with my niece. I left my son with my mother- bless his soul, while I tried to put my life back in order.

It's a shame that all the people I've helped in my life were glad to see me fall. Now, remember I was an employer and I like to think I was super good to a lot of people, but during this time I couldn't get any help from my friends or relatives. I slept on an air mattress and ate humble pie for 18 months.

July 2015, Atlanta

By this time, my money was starting to flow again so I could take care of some things that were lacking, which included housing. It felt good to be back in the privacy of my own home even if it wasn't a 5-bedroom house. Through God's grace, I had a friend who owned a small condo building he built downtown about four years ago, He allowed me to rent one of the very upscale 3 bedroom units. I had not lived in an apartment for at least 20 years, so I was feeling a certain type of way. (When I should have been feeling blessed) While I proceeded to put my life back in order, I was still sleeping on an air mattress waiting on my bonus to get the money for my pods that I had my whole life in. It was going to cost me 6 thousand dollars.

Chapter 3
The Definition of Real
Big Trouble

July 13th, 2015;

Dear God, thank you for waking me and my family today and bringing all three of my babies' home this weekend. I miss them so much, and even if we did sleep on the floor we were together. Please bless me with a nice size bonus check so I can have my pods delivered to me with all my worldly possessions. I'm thanking you in advance. Amen'

This was the **worst** day, outside of my father's death that I've ever experienced. Now, remember I told you I had an attorney who I already had on retainer in Colorado. It was a Saturday afternoon, and for some reason, this particular weekend God had all my three kids with me, and we were just chillin' out.

When my phone rang, I read my attorney´s name across my phone and for a split-second I thought about not answering it- he had always done a wellness check once or twice a month, but usually during the week, so it must have been important for him to call on the weekend.

¨Hello You¨, I said in my most bubbly voice.

He said, "Hello Capri this is your beloved attorney Mr. V" which is how he always greeted me. "However, I'm calling on a very urgent matter." What he said next made me freeze. ¨Capri you have been included in a Coca Case **indictment**."

He went on to explain that it is a conspiracy; organized crime and all what not, but I heard absolutely nothing after the word **indictment**. I sunk to the floor and cried and screamed so loud my daughter had to take the phone from me and get the rest of the information from him. She let him know that I'd call him back once she got me together.

Once the kids did finally get me back together, I came to my senses and remembered that's why I retained him and that he should be able to clear this up, with all the evidence that I had already given him, in the event something ever came up. **Right? Wrong!**

So, I finally called my attorney back, and basically felt like I was being punked and started looking around for cameras. I knew that from the day my accountant informed me about the tax preparer from Colorado there would be trouble; that was why I sought legal counsel early.

Even though I tried to do everything to protect myself, my family, business reputation, and finances. The **Government**, system or whatever entity that was in charge did not seem to care. My attorney said I would still need to turn myself in, get fingerprinted and a mugshot! I lost my mind after he said that B.S. He said "This is just how the government works." (Wow! The Mack Truck finally pushed me off the cliff)

I trusted my attorney. He was the best criminal lawyer in Colorado, Chicago and New York. He was Italian, about 70 years old, 5 ft. 7 inches tall with piercing blue eyes and looked like he just stepped out of the cover of "**I Win Every Case**" magazine. He had a 32 years old wife and 2-year-old baby. He's very well connected and super smart. I chose him after seeing his past results and getting referrals from several clients. I just kept saying, Lord please don't let anything happen to this man, and I consistently prayed for him and his family. I needed this man and hoped he would come through. *Damn! I'm just getting back on my feet, and this happens.* I seriously never in a million years thought it would get any further than my attorney's office for evidence. Especially an indictment, of all things for what? Giving this woman a job? I still did not understand how I had anything to do with her indictment, I never conspired or had any inappropriate relationship with the lady. I had only seen her maybe three or four times. The point was, I didn't care who worked for my tax business, if they knew how to process tax returns and stayed in compliance with the IRS.. As you've seen, I was far too trusting.

My attorney arraigned for me to get a bond of 250,000 dollars without going to Denver and we planned to meet with the DA to give my statement and get fingerprinted and get a mug shot). So I let my place of work know that I needed two days off so I could go and check on my mother, which was true because she had been in a car accident and was having issues. (Of course, I couldn't tell them the whole story) The plan was to turn myself in on Thursday and fly back on Sunday. My attorney suggested we would quietly handle this, so I could keep my job.

I had no idea it would still turn into a huge deal after all the actions I had taken.

Chapter 4
From Prada To Nada

On August 13TH 2015;

Dear God, please be with me today I feel like I'm about to lose my mind, I've already lost my money! Lord please speak for me and let no weapon formed against me prosper. I know that even though I am innocent that it has to be proven in the court of law, just show the evidence Lord. I'm so tired of trying to hold my head up even though I'm basically helping someone else fight a heavier war than this. Amen

I'll be flying to Colorado shortly to meet with my attorney and give my statement. Over someone else's shit! Can't wait for this to be behind me so I can continue helping my kids through school. My baby twin had already left school to come to keep an eye on me and enrolled at Georgia State to finish. I have a good job, and I don't want to lose it. I know God has this. My zombie-like state became worse with huge bags and dark marks all over my face from my nervous picking; I became a living statue. I barely ate and did not want to have conversations with anyone! I was so tired and had not slept for more than two hours at one time since this indictment. I'm headed to Denver to address this (indictment) legal issue that I have nothing to do with. I had been up in my home office all night paranoid; I told my daughter there were two cars parked facing our building, And it just felt like they were watching me. My daughter got agitated with my paranoia and said well let's just call the police; I yelled it is the police! My son and daughter dropped me off at the airport at 5 am, and they were probably glad to see me go, maybe they can get some rest now.

My other daughter is away at school but still calling all the shots. Lord God please order my footsteps and silence the negative sprit that seems to be following me, be with me through this process. Amen

Around 8 am, my daughter left my house to go to school, and my son was home by himself. BAM! BAM! BAM! My son was sleeping, he jumped up frightened and answered the door in his underwear. The fugitive squad stormed into my home. Now, this happened while I was on the plane, by the time I landed I had 500 text messages that read 'don't panic" and several missed calls from my kids. My stomach dropped down to my feet -Then I called my son. He was so shaken up that he had to put my twin daughter whom was away at college on a conference call, and she told me the S.W.A.T and the fugitive squad had been at my house.

My daughter called my attorney who in turn called the investigator that was there at my house with my son. My attorney gave them the court and bond number for verification that I was NOT a fugitive! He pleaded with them not to go to my place of work. My heart dropped as the plane pulled onto the tarmac, I was back in my zombie state again.

How the hell am I fugitive if I'm turning myself in? From that point things just spiraled out of control. I went to meet with my mom who took me to have lunch with my attorney.

Once we were done, I was interviewed and gave my statement. I could see by the look on their faces that they knew I had nothing to do with this lady's crime spree. Now, remember I barely even knew this lady other than she worked in another state under my company.

It's like they wanted me to admit something, so they kept asking me the same questions repeatedly. Although I had no idea what she had done, I was still being treated as a criminal. This one investigator from the department of revenue, I swear he looked like he was the 'Lucky Charms Leprechaun'. He was about 4'5 red hair, with freckles he asked me, "If I had any questions"? I said, "Yes. Why do you have a picture of the front of my building, where I live, in your folder?" He turned beet red and then started back peddling his words saying when he knew I was coming he called off the fugitive team. I knew he was lying and my attorney immediately laid into him, accusing him of creating this situation on purpose.

The next morning, I turned myself into the Colorado detention center. I felt like my chest was in my stomach but I had to do this to clear my name. The plan was to clear my name quickly then go turn myself in on August 14, 2015 at 4 o'clock in the morning. Since I already had a bond, all I would have to do was wait for the fingerprints to come back which normally would only take one to two hours, but suddenly that changed to 15 hours. I had to dress in jail fatigues. You could have buried me right then and there! I ended up staying there until after 7 PM in the evening! (I'll have to discuss the details of that experience in another volume)

Not long after I was released, my nephew came to pick me up. The first call I got was from my daughter in Nashville and once again she told me not to panic. After repeating "don't panic, mom" about three times, she finally explained to me that my face was all over the news in Atlanta and that the fugitive squad had been to my place of work today showing my picture all over. They even put up road blocks as if I killed someone! I just sat on the floor in the front seat of his S550 and screamed and cried. I felt like my life had ended right then, and my poor nephew tried to comfort his weak, limp, zombie of an Auntie and ended up crying too!

It was a set up, from them plotting to come to my house and knowing exactly my whereabouts, proof of my bond and guess what? They went to my place of work anyway. Even after I met with them. I came to find out they intentionally kept me in jail all that time, so they could get my mugshot and work with the authorities in Atlanta to have what my attorney called a smear campaign. Not only would my business' name be scarred but my reputation would be ruined as well.

What a waste of tax payer's money!

At that point the whole thing started sounding a bit hilarious and horrific at the same time to me. Well there goes my freaking job, and I had been killing the game in the sales department where I had only worked since February.

Folks were calling my kids all weekend being nosy, even people we hadn't heard from in like centuries still had the guts to call. Not one person was calling to offer support or financial assistance. However, when I was on top of my game I took care of everyone- and my game did not consist of stealing, or crime. I once owned a coffee bar in the prominent Buckhead area, a convenience store in Atlanta and one in Colorado, my brother and I owned a restaurant too. I had a tax business and a property management company – I have been doing taxes for a long time and as soon as I decided to hire and expand this one bad accountant initiated a years-long fiasco.

Chapter 5
Finding My Feet Again

August 18th, 2015;

*Dear God, please hear my cries and dry my tears.
I'm not sure what or who I've wronged but I know I
don't deserve this. How can I move forward Lord?
I've been used as bait, they thought I was a whale
and then found out I was just a goldfish. What will
they do to me Lord? How will I ever survive this? Oh'
God I beg of you for strength to move forward, but,
how can I? Amen*

I had to stay in Denver an extra week so that my attorney
could make sure things were cleared up in Atlanta before I
returned. It was like living in a TV movie. They ran my
mugshot all weekend long and just made things up as they
went. They even went to my old convenience store which
supposedly was where I ran my operation. My tax office
was in Roswell and I never had clients from my store come
into my office or vice versa. Things were literally just
being made up. My favorite was when they interviewed a
crack head who said he gave me $100 to do his taxes.
Needless to say, that never happened. Then reporters stood
in front of my apartment building pretending to be waiting
for me to come out. *How the hell could I walk out and they
were showing my mugshot I just took in Denver while I'm
still locked up?* It was all a setup done by Mr. Lucky
Charm and at the expense of the tax payers of Atlanta, Ga

– All freaking lies. I didn't understand why the news people didn't do their research first.

Now when I got back home I was a complete zombie. I called in sick to my job which I knew I no longer had- but just in case I followed protocol. Of course, my girlfriend from work called and asked if everything was okay. My twins talked to her while I was gone. Naturally, she wanted to know why I never said anything about what was going on. I simply said I never thought it would fester to this point, and I didn't want to be judged by someone else's wrong doing.

So of course, the banks representative called me and said they were giving me paid time off to resolve this issue, and at that point my attorney felt confident that it would be resolved quickly too. I just want to clear my name and shut these folks down, they even didn't know me or my character.

It's October 6th, 2015;

I just had a birthday On September 20TH, I still had not heard from my "Girlfriend" Mrs. C. This is someone I met at the bank, and we just clicked and became great friends, so I thought. I was beginning to worry because we used to talk every day. I have called her and sent numerous text messages to her, called her friends and I'm not sure what is going on with her. It's a mystery that someone could call themselves your friend and suddenly disappear into thin air and then to have someone else tell you that they will get in touch with you when they're available. I finally went to her house to find out what's going on. I'm what you call loyal to the end, I never thought she of all people would end up on my list of imposters. In the meantime, I've been driving Uber trying to make ends meet. I've met some incredible people these past few weeks. I need to remember to record the good things that happen every day because it helps me stay grateful, humble and thankful; and the bad things because it helps me realize that life is always a new adventure.

I did go to Mrs. C's house over a week ago, and she did not answer the door, I left her a note, and she sent me a text using someone else's phone. The text simply implied that she could not be bothered as she had a lot going on. That made me realize something else is going on, but I figured God would reveal it to me in due time. But it looks like Mrs. C was another a fair-weather friend.

Right now, I have two contracts on my properties- one person is willing to lend me money for the repairs and pay off my tax lien while the other person was going to purchase the property (her name is Mary). She called me today and said because I have a "fraud case" pending against me she could not purchase my house. Well here's an example of being "blacklisted" and I could have sued her and the company she represented. Who cares about someone's personal life if you want to purchase their property? Nobody! I've always had a great reputation in the investor community but that was all gone. It did work out anyway because (the hard money guy) had agreed to pay the small tax debt and save my house. I'm in a very good place at the moment- not the best but relatively good. I had to spend the night with my close friend Chocolate last night as she called saying she was having an anxiety attack. I wanted to say to her "boy I have those every day" but I try not to let it show. I'm a loyal friend to the end – until you cross me.

My life is just full of more downs than ups right now, and I'm doing my best to keep myself together. I'm trying not to allow this difficult time take over my life. It's hard for me to get up in the morning and hard for me to sleep at night. And in between waking up and going back to bed, my time and energy are spent on trying to figure out this thing called life and trying to breathe without suffocating myself.

Chapter 6
While I'm Waiting

October 19th 2015;

Dear God, please protect while I'm driving Uber to make ends meet. Please only bless me with people with good hearts into my car and I pray that I don't ever have to pull my gun to protect myself. I've lost my job and my dignity, but as long as there's a mint I will survive through your grace. Amen

Last week, I didn't make very much money driving Uber. I think I only made $250 while my goal is to make $500. Although I still have my rental property income thank God Mary discriminated against me and did not want to buy my house, that income has been a life saver

I must get out of the house so I drive to keep some change in my pocket and my mind from the zombie state. I sent over my tax documents and my character letters to my attorney. There is a real chance I could lose my freedom.

November 6th 2015;

I went to court in Colorado on November 6th, they had postponed it again till December 11th. I honestly believed they all just want more money; every time they postpone this crap my attorney gets money and I imagine the other attorney does too. However, it looks like they offered me a deal back in September (which I was not aware of go figure) for all charges to be dropped except for one and restitution to be split with "my codefendant" for $88,000. (Now remember I told you I sent back 88k to the IRS) I'm still trying to figure out why I got to make a deal. I just don't get it, ugghh! My attorney-says that he's been trying to get a deferred judgment. He went on to say that $30 or $40k could make all of this go away because at the end of the day it's just about money.

I got fired up to get back into real estate investment buying and selling homes. I met with my friend D.J. two weeks previous, and he put a fire underneath me. He was asking me what I had been doing and why I had not been making money because he knew how I was really good at buying and selling houses. He was right; I was sitting on my sofa just waiting for something bad to happen and that's not a good look. Anyway, now I have been blessed with a new spirit and I'm going to work while I'm waiting. I'm so happy to be in the place that I'm in at the moment- the mindset that it's time for me to get MONEY...

Chapter 7
Why This? Why Now? Why Me?

November 30th, 2015;

Dear God, thank you for giving me the breath of freedom today! I'm so grateful to know you and your miraculous works. I look forward to just another moment of not being in mental bondage. I know there's a lesson in all of this – please reveal it asap! I'm so tired. Amen

It was 3:30 in the morning. I just took Ziggy, my daughter's dog out to the bathroom. He'd been sick and trying to trick me into giving him some food but he can't have anything other than chicken broth and rice. I worked on my business plan yesterday though I couldn't get much accomplished.

I got an email from my attorney today, he sent me an attached letter ironically it was dated from September as to what the prosecutor wants from me. The plan A sounded simply horrific. However, he said he had a Plan B. My hope was that the next plan would not include money because all of it had been about money. If I had money, all of this would have been long gone. So, my plan was to make some good cash that week! I was back to my millionaire mindset. *I could not and will not be broke!*

December 11, 2015;

In Colorado once again. We had court that morning and I pleaded not guilty. I was tired of it all already. I just wanted to take the felony charge so I could get it over with even knowing I'm innocent. The government has a way of breaking you down. At this point I was tired, spent and I just wanted it to be over. My attorney would not allow me to accept a felony charge, so we were on our way to trial, unless he could get some type of agreement prior to me flying back out there February 5 to go to court again.

I had a thousand things on my mind and the first, second and third was how I had to go back home and hustle my ass off to get money to pay my attorney. My point was if it's going to be a felony later or felony now let it be a felony now, at least that way I don't have to pay any more money. It was evident that no matter how hard we tried to prove my innocence the government just wanted to pin something, anything on me. That's how I figured out how our system, which is meant to protect us-is seriously broken. It is too easy for people to get railroaded, because of lack of knowledge, funds or just simply worn out like I was. It's a shame I was willing to accept anything but jail so this episode in my life could be over.

December 22nd, 2015;

Sitting in my car praying for a miracle. I just came from the jewelry pawn shop trying to get some money. My daughter needs $230 and I have to pay my contractor who's working on my rental; I also had to pay for life insurance, health insurance, etc. But they did not want to give me what I needed, so I left the shop empty handed. I needed to make something happen and quickly. Not to mention, Christmas was a few days away. I was starting to feel very depressed. I was hoping the lender would do an $80,000 cash out on my house. *Oh, Lord, I need a miracle now!*

I'll tell you more in Volume 2.

To be continued...

Conclusion

Hello there and thank you once again for purchasing or downloading Volume 1 of the eBook "Credit Chronicles from Prada to Nada" (A Guide to Restoring Your Soul & Credit at The Same Time).

The main purpose of this book was to share with you how having good credit would have changed the whole storyline. I did not want to bore you with your same average credit guide. I wanted you recognize every time you turned the pages how my credit could have kept my life from falling apart.

Once my character was assassinated, I felt like I wasn't going to make it but as long as I prayed and realized that my lesson wasn't about the situation I was going through, it was about what I had not done with the blessings God had already bestowed upon me. The one lesson I kept coming back to was my credit. I want you to know that every day you should work on your credit and your spirit, taking both to the next level

This book was written for those who are not aware of the importance of having good credit; and a well-balanced spiritual soul also for those who are aware but have yet to start making the right moves and for those who are getting it right. If you enjoyed Volume 1 of this book, believe me when I say you will be super charged after Volume 2. It's loaded with another exciting story to share with you and more insightful credit tips - that will refresh your, soul, mind and credit.

What's next? The following 7 mini-credit steps will help you start putting all you have read into practice and recommend this book to those you love so they can be empowered too.

Remember to start living well and start restoring your soul and credit today.

NEVER LET YOUR PAST DICTATE YOUR FUTURE!

7 mini-STEPS that have huge impact

STEP 1 – GET EDUCATED- UNDERSTAND WHY YOU NEED CREDIT

- Get a copy of your Credit Report from all 3 bureaus- Trans Union, Equifax, and Experian and get familiar with them!

- If you are checking your credit history for the first time, by law, you're entitled to receive a free copy of your credit report from Equifax, Experian and TransUnion once every 12 months.

- Get your score! Your credit score is not included with your free credit report. But you have a number of ways to get a score at no cost.

  (I'll give you all the resources you need at the end of this book)

- Maintaining good credit is one of the best things you can do to keep financially healthy. A strong credit history and credit score can help you get better interest rates on loans, credit cards, and lines of credit. Plus, many insurance companies, cell phone providers, and landlords refer to your credit score to make decisions. Your credit activity, or what you borrow and when you repay it, make up your credit history.

- Credit reporting agencies collect this information from various sources and issue reports based on your borrowing and debt-paying habits. All this information contributes to your credit score, which is like a grade for your credit report.

- Your credit history determines what loans you will qualify for and the interest rate you will pay. Lenders get your credit history by obtaining your credit score. You'll most likely need to borrow funds from a lender. Therefore credit is such an important component to the home buying process.

- Your creditworthiness is defined by your three-digit credit score and is the key to your financial life. Good credit can be the make-or-break detail that determines whether you'll get a mortgage, car loan or student loan.

- Good credit -can signify that your financial situation - and the rest of your life - is headed in the right direction.

– RESTORE YOUR SOUL

While educating yourself, and learning all about your credit and how it affects you, drink a hot cup of green tea.

Here's why –

This makes a difference because green tea contains significant quantities of *theanine*, a compound that has considerable stress-reducing effects. In fact, it has been shown that *theanine* reduces physiological responses to stress, such as the heart rate. To be frank, your credit report can stress you out, so trust me you'll need the tea!

Personal Note: Did you notice that in chapter 1 I never mentioned anything about credit, exercise, having a healthy diet or anything like that? Well to me these things weren't important then. All that was important to me were surviving and staying afloat in life and business. I was not taking care of myself and wasn't even thinking about my credit. In fact, at the time I didn't even know what my credit report or score was. I was too busy trying to ask God why he was punishing me at such a rapid pace.

STEP 2 —AUDIT YOUR CREDIT REPORTS CAREFULLY KNOW WHAT TO LOOK FOR:

Keep in mind that credit report data originates from the companies who have accounts with you. The objective is to correct your credit report, as well as to ensure that your information is and the report line up.

Grab a sheet of paper and write down every incorrect piece of information in the report. Believe me, there will always be a mistake or two so do it diligently. Here's where you must start. The order here is important.

- **Personal Identification (addresses, employment history, name, social security number)**

- **Types of Accounts (revolving, installment, loans, joint accounts, credit limits, debts)**

- **Collections (if any accounts went to collections)**

- **Public Records (about financial obligations)**

- **Consumer Statement (such as a statement of dispute if you do not agree with your lender about the status of your account)**

- **Hard Credit Inquiries (showing you applied for new credit or services)**

- **Soft Credit Inquiries (showing requests made by lenders who sent you an offer or that you requested your own report — soft inquiries are shown only to you)**

AUDIT AND REPAIR. NOW'S THE TIME, DON'T WAIT UNTIL THE CHIPS FALL *I'll give you some tips in the back of this book that could boost your credit score by 50-70 points by only making 1 secret correction.*

– RESTORE YOUR SOUL

While you are performing your audit, play some good music, like some jazz or something smooth so you can relax and concentrate.

Here's why:

Music gives you the freedom to be who you are or who you want to be. Not what the Credit Bureaus want you to be. Yes, get in a good mood because you are on your way to financial paradise.

Personal Note:

Did you notice in chapter 2 once again I never mentioned credit, exercise, healthy diet or anything! Because I still was not taking care of my spiritual self. I assumed my credit was not up to par to even get an apartment, so I didn't even try to look for one. **POINT:** *I should have known what I could and could not obtain credit-wise, here's another example of lack of credit knowledge. If I was educated regarding my credit, I could have gotten a line of credit and received my pods and apartment with no problem.*

STEP 3 – LEARN! LEARN!! LEARN!!! ALL ABOUT CREDIT SCORES (CHANGE YOUR SCORE, CHANGE YOUR LIFE)

DO YOU NEED TO BUILD OR REPAIR YOUR CREDIT?

- If your credit score is over 700, then you probably have a good understanding of how credit works.

- If your credit score is below 700, then you need to analyze it and see where to improve it.

- If your credit score is below 600, you need to repair and build!

When working to fix your credit score, remember that taking short-cuts usually leads to potholes in the future. It may take time, but patience and persistence will be helpful to you. ***Also, beware of fix-credit-quick advice***.

– RESTORE YOUR SOUL

Patience and persistence require calmness and composure. Regardless of how your scores might be looking do not beat yourself up. Take time to ensure that your body is calm. One easy way to achieve this is by practicing deep breathing- "whole body breathing"

It requires daily conscious effort. Inhale and exhale ensuring that you feel every breath, ensuring that all cells and tissues within your body feel each breath.

POINT: *Had I taken the time learn or research who I was allowing to infiltrate my business then I would have made a different decision.*

Personal Note:

Still in chapter 3, I hadn't gotten a grip of how important my credit was or how important exercise, breathing, eating healthy and all that good stuff were. These benefits would be felt not only by my body but my soul and spirit. I was still had a lot to learn.

STEP 4 - KNOW WHAT IMPACTS YOUR CREDIT RATING

There are five factors that affect your credit score rating. They are (from most to least important)

- Your payment history. (35%)

  This describes whether you are able to repay money lent to you and is dependent on your past history (how soon were you able to pay up). Late payment of bills (and how late you paid) also negatively affects this parameter. Other things include your bankruptcies, liens, foreclosures and any charge-offs.

- Amounts owed. (30%)

  This describes how much you have owed. It considers how much of your total credit has been used. For this, the less you have used the better. But remember that doesn't mean you shouldn't borrow at all as lenders are interested in knowing how quickly you are able to pay up after taking a loan. Other factors that are considered include how much you owe on different accounts, how much you owe in general and how close you are to your limit.

- Length of your credit history. (15%)

  This considers how long you have been using your account. For this, the longer the better. A long history without late payments is a deal breaker.

- Number of new accounts. (10%)

  This considers how many new accounts you have opened or applied for lately. The reason this is important is because it is assumed that the more accounts you have opened recently, the greater the possibility that you have been having cash flow problems.

- Types of credit you have. (10%)

  This considers the total number of accounts you have and the different kinds of credit you have including mortgages, credit cards, and installment loans.

RESTORE YOUR SOUL

Try to get as much sleep as you can. A lack of sleep leads to the release of a substance called ghrelin. This substance is what makes you feel hungrier every time you aren't getting enough sleep. How long is good enough for you? At least 6 hours at night time, regardless of what's on your mind, what you must do or what is stressing you. Chamomile tea is great for you if you can't find it in yourself to sleep. Take a bath, and observe a bedtime routine every night (always at the same time). Ensure that your bed isn't another work zone for you- ensure there are no blinking or bright lights around you especially those from your devices and that you stop reading or writing at least 15 minutes before your intended sleep time. Turn off all lights or use an eye mask to block out the light. Also, use earplugs if you are in a "noisy" environment.

Personal Note:

As you guessed, I still hadn't gotten a grip on why credit was important to me. Neither had I had the time for eating healthy, exercising or breathing deeply or doing all that good stuff. Being credit wise would have provided me with several doorways to get out of the mess I was in. If only I had known.

POINT: If my instincts were only as good as my hustle skills I would have never been in this situation, the same goes for your credit- don't assume. Always investigate the situation!

STEP 5 - KNOW THE DO'S AND DON'TS WHEN IT COMES TO YOUR CREDIT

- Do use a credit card instead of a debit card

- Do check your credit history

- Do use the right card at the right time

- Do take out time to fix all credit report errors

- Do apply for and open credit accounts only when needed

- Do ask for redress if you miss a payment

- Don't eat too deep into your available balance

- Don't close old or unused credit cards

- Don't move your debts around- pay them off.

- Don't miss your payments

RESTORE YOUR SOUL

A thousand and one activities will be thrown at you, do not let them sway you. Stay focused! There will be a few inevitable things you would need to handle in life, some of these may include bad debt or delaying payments, fix them now. The "that's a done deal" feeling will provide you and your soul with peace- though it may be short-lived it would do you a lot of good.

Personal Note:

Chapter 5 revealed a version of me simply trying to hang on in life. I was struggling to stay afloat- yes, I seemed to be doing better, but inwardly and outwardly I was drained. I had lost track of what it meant to live a fulfilled life simply because I was aware that there was a better way to live- a wiser way to live. If only I had known about the importance of credit scores.

POINT: Had I been on top of my own business instead of trying to make sure everyone else was okay then once again, I would have never been in this place! So-called friends can ride or die but will only ride until they've taken all you have and decide to forget all about the "die" part.

STEP 6 - STOP THE PROCRASTINATION START THE REPAIR PROCESS

- What Mindset Do You Have?

  - Do you believe you have money, so you do not need credit?

  - Do you believe that if you can't pay cash for it, then you do not need it?

These were two of the numerous wrong mentalities I possessed. When I needed a loan, I couldn't get one because I had no credit. I had paid cash for my cars, I purchased my house before I became financially successful, my insurance rates, life and auto, went up when I renewed my policies- and I could not understand why? – MY CREDIT!!! Having cash and no credit is DUMB!

- Have the "I can do it" mentality.

What do you have to do to start fixing your credit score? What steps do you have to take? Are you ready? If no, why not?! Procrastination has never done anyone any good. Start today!

RESTORE YOUR SOUL

Nourish your body by eating healthy meals. A thousand and one billboards and adverts advise us to stay healthy by eating healthy yet still a thousand and one of them teach us otherwise. Remember it's your body, so it's your call. Make the wise decision.

Personal Note:

Chapter 6 revealed the version of me that was ready to pick up the pieces by working hard to put my kids through school and to enjoy life as much as I could. This was still a version of me that was oblivious to the importance of credit and credit scores. Hence I struggled where I could be soaring and settled for less when I could be living in plenty.

STEP 7 - STAYING AT THE TOP OF THE LADDER (HOW TO MAINTAIN GOOD CREDIT)

Maintaining good credit is a lifelong process. You would need consistency and hard work but it would be well worth it. It first starts with making a conscious decision to stay at the top of the ladder and follow that decision through to the letter. Ensure you pay your bills on time even if it would require setting up payment reminders for yourself. Ensure you reduce the amount of debt that you owe and settle all debts before the expiration date. A conscious effort is what is needed for you to maintain a good credit score. One last thing... Believe you can do it, because you can.

RESTORE YOUR SOUL

Would this book be complete if I fail to mention exercise and its importance? Integrating movement into your day can help you restore not only your body but your soul and spirit. Try some yoga stretches and light walking. Swimming is always great for you. Remember, if it feels right for your body, it probably is.

Personal Note:

Up until then all that I could think about was what I was going through at that point in time. But seeing things in retrospect always gives us a wider view, and now I know better.

POINT: *Credit = CASH!*

Let's Recap What You've Learned:

- You've Pulled Your Credit, Right? Write down three things you learned.

  _____

  _____

  _____

  _____

- What is the first thing on your credit report you need to verify?

  _____

  _____

  _____

  _____

- What are your credit scores with all 3 bureaus?

  Equifax_____ needs improvement? _____

  TransUnion_____ needs improvement? _____

  Experian_____ needs improvement? _____

- Why should you maintain good credit?

  _____

  _____

  _____

  _____

- What are the main 2 requirements you must have to restore and elevate your credit score?

  _____

  _____

  _____

  _____

The Resources I promised:

Free Credit Reports

You are entitled to a free credit report from each of the three credit reporting agencies (Equifax, Experian, and TransUnion) once every 12 months. You can request all three reports at once, or space them out throughout the year. Learn about other situations in which you can request a free credit report.

Request your free credit report:

Online: Visit AnnualCreditReport.com

By Phone: Call 1-877-322-8228. Deaf and hard of hearing consumers can access the TTY service by calling 711 and referring the Relay Operator to 1-800-821-7232.

By Mail: Complete the Annual Credit Report Request Form (PDF, Download Adobe Reader) and mail it to:

Annual Credit Report Request Service
PO Box 105281
Atlanta, GA 30348-5281

To get your credit score you can go to: These all offer tri-merge reports so just go to one of them.

www.equifax.com

www.myfico.com

www.creditchecktotal.com

www.transunion.com

HERE'S SOME BANKS TO HELP THOSE IN CHEXSYSTEMS;

BANK RESOURCE PAGE

If Chex Systems has you blocked from getting a checking account here are some banks they don't use Chex Systems:

Woodforest National Bank

Woodforest National Bank, a regional financial institution, also offers a Second Chance Checking account to customers with a history of banking problems. However, you must apply in person. Keep in mind that:

- A minimum of $25 is required to open an account.

- There is a monthly fee of $9.95 with direct deposit or $11.95 without it

- Woodforest National Bank is located in select states, including: Alabama, Florida, Georgia, Kentucky, Louisiana, Illinois, Indiana, Maryland, Mississippi, New York, North Carolina, Ohio, Pennsylvania, South Carolina, Texas, Virginia and West Virginia

United Bank

A bad ChexSystems report is not a problem with United Bank. However, the bank has limited locations in Washington, D.C., Virginia, Ohio, Maryland and Pennsylvania. Features and requirements of this account include:

- $50 minimum opening deposit

- Free United Visa CheckCard

- No monthly fees

Southwest Financial Federal Credit Union

Don't want to fuss with paper checks? The Texas-based <u>Southwest Financial Federal Credit Union</u> offers a Checkless Checking account. It's perfect for individuals who previously couldn't qualify for bank accounts. Features and requirements include:

- Free debit card

- No monthly service fees

- A required savings account

Wells Fargo

<u>Wells Fargo</u> has a big heart, offering Second Chance checking to customers with a negative ChexSystems report. Called an Opportunity Checking account, it includes everything you expect from a basic checking account, from online banking to easy bill pay. However, you'll have to open the account at a local branch. Your account will come with:

- $10 monthly fee, which can be waived if you make 10 debit card purchases, maintain a $1,500 daily balance or post a total of $500 in direct deposits per statement cycle

- Minimum opening deposit is $50

PNC Bank

Another big bank that offers Second Chance checking to customers with a bad banking report is PNC, which offers Foundation Checking. This account is for customers who want to re-establish themselves in the banking world. You'll have to open an account in person after taking and passing an online Foundations of Money Management Course. Your account will also come with:

- $7 monthly service charge

- $2 fee for paper statements

- After 6 months or longer, you might be eligible for other accounts

Capital One

Although the Capital One 360 account does consider your ChexSystems report, Capital One doesn't base approval on ChexSystems alone. Therefore, it's still possible to be approved for a Capital One 360 account. Chances are, if you have a decent credit score and no banking fraud, you'll be golden.

- No fees or minimums

- Free MasterCard Debit Card

Renasant Bank

This bank is only located in Mississippi, Alabama, Tennessee, and Georgia. You can have a Chexsystems, Telecheck or EWS record but there must not be any money owed to Renasant

Bank. Checking accounts offer free online bill pay along with mobile banking. You can apply online.

BBVA Compass NBA Free Checking

Available to residents in ALL States is the BBVA NBA Checking Account. BBVA Compass is a No-ChexSystems Bank. Show support for your NBA team with a Visa debit card displaying your favorite team. There is no monthly fee plus you get mobile check deposits, bill pay and check writing. If you are not eligible, you will be offered the Second Chance Checking Account with the same features including a Visa debit card, but there is a $13.95 monthly fee. The second chance account is offered when you need to rebuild credit and get your finances on track.

Fort Sill National Bank

Fort Sill National Bank (FSNB) is open to anyone — you do not have to be in the military. FSNB does not use ChexSystems. If you are interested in direct deposit, this may be a good account for you because FSNB may not be in your state. In order to open an account from any location call their new accounts department at (800) 749-4583 and an application will be mailed to you

1st Convenience Bank

This bank is only located in New Mexico, Texas, and Arizona. They do not run Chexsystems, Telecheck, or EWS. Several checking account options are available but there is a $12 monthly maintenance fee if certain conditions are not met such as maintaining a minimum daily balance. All checking account options only require $1.00 to open

THESE ARE TIPS TO INCREASE YOUR CREDIT SCORE

FICO, the Fair Isaac Corporation, is the overwhelming credit scoring company, serving each bank, loan specialist, and budgetary association with its credit reporting of a huge number of Americans. Even though they might be profoundly noticeable as the monster in the business, they're to a great degree hidden with regards to how they compute your financial assessments. While we do know when all is said in done what aides or damages your score and the weighted rates that go into their computations, FICO keeps its calculations a firmly protected industry mystery.

Nonetheless, there are a few pieces of data that have been spilled by FICO workforce or uncovered by industry insiders. A hefty portion of their practices are questionable. Some have even been called "marginal conning" by FICO due to the fact that they are so successful, yet they assert that they're all lawful.

Obviously we recommend you adopt mindful and judicious budgetary practices – like keeping up a low obligation load, paying every one of your bills on time, and so forth to lawfully and morally raise FICO ratings, however, it's certainly helpful to know there are a couple of FICO assessment hacks to help your score.

Here are 9 insights to build your FICO rating:

1. **Turn into an approved client on another person's MasterCard.**

   Maybe the most proficient approach to building your financial assessment in a short time is by turning into an approved client on another person's charge card. Once you're approved, the new positive exchange line will appear on your credit as though you've had it since the card had been issued. It's essential you do this accurately – it must be a credit line in extraordinarily good standing. Moreover, it ought to be somebody you trust well (and they trust you!) because if the essential client keeps running up enormous obligations, has late installments, or defaults, you'll be on the snare and your credit will really be harmed. Be that as it may, FICO knows a great deal of guardians do this to build their youngster or matured kids' credit – and it's a perfectly lawful practice.

2. Demand an expansion (with no aim of utilizing it.)

One way a few people attempt to build their FICO rating is by expanding their obligation to accessible equalization proportion. In any case, rather than paying down their obligation dependably (which is suggested!) they call their charge cards and other spinning obligation loan bosses and demand a credit line increment. On the off chance that in truth, their proportions look much better to FICO without having paid a dime off their parity!

3. Report your card lost.

This mystery strategy was spilled by an abnormal state FICO representative. With the objective of including an extra constructive exchange line (without applying anywhere or regardless of the possibility that you can't qualify) a few people call their lenders and report their charge card stolen. At the point when that happens, they will generally close that record and open another record and move most of your financial record over to the new one – including the first open date. Viola! You now have two positive and prepared credit lines where there was only one before.

4. Deny, deny, deny.

With regards to little records that harm your FICO rating – an unpaid stopping ticket, a doctor's visit expense that you neglected to pay on time, or a miniscule parity on an old PDA – it bodes well to question them with the credit authorities. Since the obligations are little and old, the organizations and loan bosses will probably not in any case bother with the expense of trying to collect on them. Consequently, by denying they exist or that they are accurate you'll likely get some negative "stays" off your credit report.

5. Include MIA accounts.

A surefire approach to build your credit is to include positive records that aren't right now being accounted for. Even though FICO doesn't effectively advertise this data, you can do that by asking for unreported records to be considered your credit. Consider any organization that pulls your credit and to which you pay your bills on time. Case in point, mobile phones, Internet suppliers, service organizations, and therapeutic billers frequently don't try reporting credit (since it's not compulsory.) But rather on the off chance that you request that they do as such, they well may go along – posting a very well prepared, positive new exchange line on your FICO rating. Blast!

6. "Influence" your leasers.

Obviously you shouldn't fix anybody, however that is a term FICO utilizes freely for customers who arrange "Pay for cancellation." If you've missed enough installments to have a record in accumulations, they'll frequently consent to delete any negative credit reporting for that record on the off chance that you fork over the required funds. Ensure you get their guarantee in writing and you'll presumably need to make a singular amount installment, yet the uplifting news is that collecting organizations regularly settle for a smaller rate of your total obligation (since they paid pennies on the dollar for it.)

7. Eradicate the proof.

With more understudy advances going into default in view of unemployment, titanic understudy advance equalizations for graduates, or simply the high average cost for basic items, the harm of a missed installment can hit your FICO assessment hard. Yet, don't be alarmed – there is an alternative to get the negative reporting deleted from your credit report *if* you restore the obligation. That implies organizing an arrangement with your moneylender to convey the installments cutting-edge. When you make 9 out of 10 installments on time, there is a one-time exception (just with Federal advances) that they'll eradicate the harm from your credit.

8. Figure out the mystery Report Date code.

Obviously, it's simple for shoppers to know when their Visa or advance's due is and pay on time, however there is another number you ought to know about. Every lender likewise has a Report Date – when they send their data into the credit authorities and FICO. On the off chance that you utilize your MasterCard a ton and pay it off at the due date, the higher parity will dependably appear on your credit report that month since Report Date is before Due Date. So, an insider tip to build FICO assessment is to call your lender, ask them what day they report, and try to pay your records off or down before that date – not the due date.

9. Think lower.

FICO figures a critical bit of your score by your credit use proportion – how much obligation you keep to how much your aggregate accessible equalizations are. Normal exhortation is that you ought to keep that proportion at or underneath 30% ($3,000 of obligation for a MasterCard with $10,000 accessible. In any case, FICO insiders now admit that 20% or even the distance down to 10% or less are shockingly better proportions to keep up, and will support your score. Nonetheless, don't go the distance to 0% in light of the fact that it won't demonstrate a set up installment history they can use in their estimations (you won't have any installments.)

Great Websites for Credit information:

www.ftc.gov

www.thecreditchronicles.com   Start your credit freedom at my site for only $9.99 go here for my DIY program complete with dispute letters, tips on how to remove bankruptcy, tax liens, medical bills Quick! Be one of the few to join the 700+ club!

www.freescoreonline.com

www.ftccomplaintassistant.gov

www.annualcreditreport.com

Motivational &Inspirational Reads/Videos

The Bible

God's Ancient Secret, Peter Popoff

Think and Grow Rich, Napoleon Hill

Proverbs for Business, Steve Mar

Instinct, TD Jakes

48 Laws of Power, Robert Greene

Conspiracy of Credit, Corey P. Smith

TD Jakes – Youtube videos

Les Brown – Youtube videos

Emani Turnage
copy of Test - covid
Leave →

march 1 → }

Made in the USA
Columbia, SC
23 July 2019